A Dog Lover's Devotional

A Dog Lover's Devotional

31 Daily Walks with God and Your Dog

RON NEISH

XULON PRESS

Xulon Press
2301 Lucien Way #415
Maitland, FL 32751
407.339.4217
www.xulonpress.com

Paperback ISBN-13: 978-1-66286-611-1
Ebook ISBN-13: 978-1-66286-612-8

TABLE OF CONTENTS

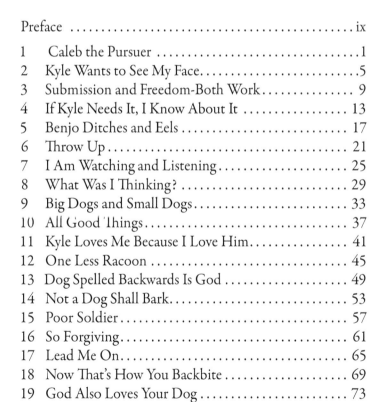

PREFACE

This book uses some experiences with dogs to meditate on some challenges that relate to our pursuit of God. None of the analogies in this devotional are meant to be perfect Scriptural parallels. They are simple observations that may cause us to think a little deeper about a Bible verse, a quality of our God, or an area of our lives where we can do better.

Anything good that might have come from this book in your life came from the Creator of Kyle, Ellie, Josi, Dusty, and Tinker—the dogs I was blessed to have in my life. I also mention two dogs I have spent many hours with, Tag and Jersey, who are close to me through family members.

I am sorry if you are disappointed that this devotional does not include cats. I can only think to refer you to C.S. Lewis' *Screwtape Letters* to fill that void.

Surely none of the men who came up from Egypt,
from twenty years old and above, shall see the land of which I
swore to Abraham, Isaac, and Jacob,
*because they have **not wholly followed** Me,*
'except Caleb the son of Jephunneh, the Kenizzite,
and Joshua the son of Nun, for they have
***wholly followed** the LORD.*
(Numbers 32:11-12 emphasis added)

"I want the presence of God Himself, or I don't want any-
thing at all to do with religion...
I want all that God has or I don't want any."
— A.W. Tozer[1]

Caleb the Pursuer

I visited a mid-week service at Calvary Chapel in East Anaheim Hills and listened to a lesson about Caleb. The pastor summarized the familiar story of Caleb and Joshua, the only two spies sent into the Promised Land who did not come back doubting God's directive to conquer it. Those two men did not return shaking in fear of the giants in the land. Rather, they celebrated Almighty God who would rout their enemies and give the Israelites a land flowing with milk and honey.

The speaker masterfully painted a word picture of Caleb, the dog, pursuing God. Years later, I was with my wife, kids, and my nephew Caleb at the Richard Nixon Library where we met a Jewish man, Michael Medved, who focused our brief meeting on my nephew's name. Michael pronounced it in Hebrew and told him that the meaning of his name, dog, carried no insult to the religious Jew, but great respect. It makes sense that the name would be associated with honor.

Notice the words "wholly followed" or "wholeheartedly followed" in another translation of Numbers 32:11-12.

This is where my dog, Kyle, enters the picture.

Clearly, God was not pleased His people did not wholly follow Him, but was very pleased that Caleb wholeheartedly did so. What does it mean to "wholeheartedly follow" God? It is easy to read a verse or a well-known Bible story in a lazy fashion.

The picture of wholly following God might look like someone who really has their act together - devotions, church, prayer, etc. However, thanks to good sermons, a man named Caleb, and our dogs, perhaps we can all be a little humbled at what "wholeheartedly following" God can look like.

We do not want to fool ourselves into thinking we are wholeheartedly following God if we are not. Our devotions, listening to Christian radio, and ministering at the local rescue mission are all good.

However, I must ask myself how often or if ever I resemble Kyle chasing a rabbit. When Kyle chases a rabbit, there is never a question about whether he gave it his all.

Now, if a dog can be "all in" over a rabbit, shouldn't we be showing that same passion as pursuers of God?

Father, I admit my pursuit of You is not what it could be and I thank You for Your grace. May looking at Caleb and other examples of pursuing You humble me. Grant me the strength and courage to follow You wholeheartedly all the time and in everything I say or do. Lord, examine my heart and help me to be "all in." Make it clear how I can passionately and completely be surrendered to Your will and ways. Amen.

So the LORD said to Moses, "I will also do this thing that you have spoken; for you have found grace in My sight, and I know you by name." And he said, "Please, show me Your glory." Then He said, "I will make all My goodness pass before you, and I will proclaim the name of the LORD before you.... But He said, "You cannot see My face; for no man shall see Me, and live.... Here is a place by Me, and you shall stand on the rock. So it shall be, while My glory passes by, that I will put you in the cleft of the rock, and will cover you with My hand while I pass by. Then I will take away My hand, and you shall see My back; but My face shall not be seen." (Exodus 33:17-23)

"Prayer is beyond any question the highest activity of the human soul. Man is at his greatest and highest when upon his knees he comes face to face with God."
— D. Martin Lloyd-Jones[2]

-2-

KYLE WANTS TO SEE MY FACE

Have you ever laid down with your dog and hid your face? If I lie down and hide my face, Kyle is not happy. I have seen this with other dogs, so I know it is not uncommon. Your dog wants to see your face. If I bury my face, I will feel a wet nose go under my neck that pushes my head up, or I experience many sloppy licks to the neck until Kyle can see my face. He gets all excited to see my face again. Like, "Phew, where were you? I didn't like that."

He will particularly do this if I prompt him to interact with me, such as when I lay down with him and grab at his paws or ears to start a play session. Engaging him and prompting him for interaction, I stir up a lot within him. If I then hide my face, Kyle wants to see my face even more.

This little idiosyncrasy of a dog leads us to a wonderful meditation on Scripture.

In Exodus 33:11, we read, "So the LORD spoke to Moses face to face, as a man speaks to his friend..." This apparent conflict leads to a study of the Hebrew word *paniym* translated into English as "face." This word can be used in both figurative and factual ways.

We know God has shown Himself in other forms other than in His full glory where people could see His face (like Jesus). So, the use of the word *paniym* has not created insurmountable conflict, but actually leads to a deeper reading of scripture and more meditation on God.

It is not wrong to *want* to see the very face of God or the fullness of His glory. God did not say Moses' request was wrong, but He knew the limits of Moses as a human.

In 2 Chronicles 7:14, the Lord said, "if My people who are called by My name will humble themselves, and pray and seek My face, and turn from their wicked ways, then I will hear from heaven, and will forgive their sin and heal their land."

God clearly wants us to seek His face. What a personal and intimate desire laid before us. An omnipotent God uses His own face to help us understand how relational He is. He could have said, "I want you to hang around Me, follow Me, and obey Me."

All of which would have been good to hear. However, this reference to His *paniym* is like a love letter.

When we fall in love on earth, we yearn for that person to want to be with us "face-to-face." We want that person to meet our eyes. God knows that He and He alone can bring healing to His people. It is *His* face our hearts should be longing to see. He knows that only seeking His face can bring us the joy and fullness we need. No idol formed by man can cut it. No man or woman can compete with the face of God. Certainly, no pagan custom or practice can compare to the face of God.

Father, we want to see Your face. We long to see Your eyes and Your smile. We long to see You look at us. Jesus, we rejoice in knowing that one day we will see You face-to-face.

*What fruit did you have then in the things of which you are now ashamed? For the end of those things is death. But now having been **set free from sin**, and having **become slaves of God**, you have your fruit to holiness, and the end, everlasting life.*
(Romans 6:21-22 emphasis added)

"In almost everything that touches our everyday life on earth, God is pleased when we're pleased. He wills that we be as free as birds to soar and sing our maker's praise without anxiety."
— A. W. Tozer[3]

SUBMISSION AND FREEDOM
– BOTH WORK
KYLE AND TINKER

S uggesting that submission and freedom go together risks sounding like a slogan from Orwell's 1984, where all people are equal, but some people are more equal than others.

Kyle and Tinker may help us meditate on how submitting to a sovereign loving God can lead us to a maximum level of divinely provided freedom. So, I begin my Tale of Two Dogs (pun reluctantly intended) that is not meant to be a perfect analogy for the above verse, but could provide some related perspective.

Tinker was the most "unsubmitted" pet dog I have ever known, and Kyle was the most submissive I have ever owned. Tinker lived in bondage and Kyle lived in relative freedom. Let's look at this. We got Tinker while we lived in Okinawa. Tinker's breed was, as far as we could tell, a pariah. She never really claimed us. In fact, it took about fourteen years to learn she was likely not a breed that could be fully domesticated. Tinker would dash out of the front door every chance she got. Imagine unwittingly owning a coyote, and you are close.

The very idea of taking her to a park and playing fetch off leash was out of the question as she would no doubt have run away (we tried). She would have quickly been among the many road kills that were prevalent on Okinawan streets.

Our family paid to take this disloyal animal back to the U.S. in 1975. You didn't read about a dog falling from a high-rise hotel in downtown Los Angeles that day for only one reason. My dad shut a balcony door quickly enough when he heard the sound of Tinker running behind him. So strong was her desire to be free that she would have vaulted to her death.

Life in our home meant monitoring Tinker closely. Often another family member had to be called just to hold her by the collar if someone needed to leave the house or open the door to a visitor. We lived in an "all-hands-on-deck" mentality.

Now, Kyle? I let Kyle run free on every walk. He could hang out on the front lawn. Often, I would let him be a hundred yards away from me sniffing and chasing and digging because he knew to return.

I loved Kyle; therefore, I had no desire to rule over him like a crazed authoritarian. I needed him to obey me, but I also wanted him to enjoy the freedom to explore and be a dog. My brother-in-law, the golfer, would sometimes smack a golf ball deep into the woods on family walks and Kyle would retrieve it. Kyle could barely maintain himself on the back swing knowing he was about to chase and hunt. Tinker would have run the other way and joined a pack of coyotes.

My father grew up in a ranch environment and had a border collie. His dog would get up at a certain time each evening to bring in the sheep. To do this he actually went over hills and out of sight. No one went with him; he just knew it was time, got up, left, and herded sheep back close to the home. Every evening. Every day.

Ask a mature Christian if they feel God is leashing them. Their answer may likely be "no." Or ask a missionary if they felt "I gotta go there? Share Christ with them? Ugh!" These folks tend sheep and seek sheep because they love the sheep. They love the sheep because they love the Shepherd. So, tending to them has become what they are now "bred" to do. So yes, the freedom in this verse relates to being set free from the bondage of sin, but being free from that bondage makes us free in other ways.

Do you have a nagging suspicion you should be doing something, but you are not because it feels like you will be strapped to this "thing" and it will rule you? Are you a mom whose own children have left home and this unwed mother ministry keeps pricking your heart to join? Is there a neighbor that you know you should reach out to? You want to be a volunteer at the hospital, but…

When we are not appreciating and enjoying our freedom from the slavery of sin, perhaps our minds are not allowing us to follow our new "breeding" where we can't wait to "slave" away at the Master's tasks for us.

Father, may I not follow You or do acts of service with the wrong attitude. May You so infuse me with the joy of my salvation and the renewing of my mind that I use my freedom wisely for Your name's sake.

Cast your burden on the LORD,
And He shall sustain you;
He shall never permit the righteous to be moved.
(Psalm 55:22)

Therefore humble yourselves under the mighty
hand of God, that He may exalt you in due time, casting all
your care upon Him, for He cares for you.
(1 Peter 5:6-7)

"Cast your cares on God; that anchor holds."
— Frank Moore Colby

-4-

IF KYLE NEEDS IT, I KNOW ABOUT IT

People can be very hesitant to bring their needs before God. There are reasons for this, and those reasons should concern us. Many, without realizing it, don't want to admit there is a God more powerful than them and that they actually need Him. Sometimes, folks don't care enough about their own needs, like overcoming a sin, so are not as passionate about putting those sins to death as they should be. We can see a need, but often we don't care enough about the need to be on our knees. Perhaps, we sometimes are blind to Scripture, and we are not hearing God speak. Failing to bring our concerns and prayers to God is failing to listen to God.

> *"If you then, being evil, know how to give good gifts to your children, how much more will your Father who is in heaven give good things to those who ask Him!* (Matthew 7:11)

My truck has a fold-down center console and Kyle rides in the back cab area. I rest my arm on the center console as I drive. Well, at least I try to rest my arm. What actually happens is I get a wet nose under my forearm and a sudden flip that results in my arm not so subtly being put in a position to pet him. Actually, he is too close to pet comfortably so I must pull my shoulder away to pet him, and it is never comfortable. Now, one would think I would resent this. I mean, here I am riding along, deep in thought, with my arm comfortably resting on the console. And now it is cocked backward and petting a needy dog that demands my hand on him.

I am not really a "good guy." I have met some really great and nice people, but let's just be kind and give me an average grade. But even with that average grade, I don't scold Kyle for seeking my attention. In fact, I know my dog so well, let me speak for him. "Gosh, thanks for letting me come along. I love being in the truck with you. Especially because I am pretty sure I know where we are going and it is great there. But to really make this complete, can you get your hand on me? Ah, that's it. And yes, specifically if you could massage that part of my upper shoulder as you drive that would really make this whole thing complete. Because, gosh, I really love having your hand on me. It's awesome."

Kyle doesn't hide his hunger, either. Kyle, like so many dogs, has a very accurate watch when it comes to being fed. He knows mealtime almost to the minute. He stares at me expectantly. If I am inside, a few bumps on the sliding door with his nose serves as a very clear message-I am hungry.

So how receptive is God to my nudges and my desire to have His hand on me? I say my prayers, read the Bible, and try to be a good family man, but rarely do I take all my cares to the

Lord. But then I think of Kyle and agree, "Yeah, that would be so good to have God's hand on me right now. I would love that. If Kyle can get my attention, what is stopping me from going deeper with my requests to feel His love upon me more and more."

Father, let us not be shy to bring our requests before You. Give us wisdom about what we should be praying for and clean hearts and motives so that our petitions may be brought in truth.

Nor shall you bring an abomination into your house, lest you be doomed to destruction like it. You shall utterly detest it and utterly abhor it, for it is an accursed thing. (Deuteronomy 7:26)

BENJO DITCHES AND EELS

Tinker, our Okinawan pariah dog, and escape artist had strange tastes. When she ran away from us in Okinawa, upon her return she smelled bad. Real bad.

The better of the two main smells she returned with was that of fish - eels specifically. We didn't live close to the ocean, but we lived near an eel farm. The eel farm in Okinawa was more akin to a dirty pool. It would look a lot like an X-file episode if someone fell in it. Somehow, this little wild dog would get into the facility and either find a trashcan of dead eels to roll in, or maybe she actually caught those delicacies somehow. We all knew her well enough not to put anything past her. We never figured that one out. She did have eel breath with the eel slime on her fur, though. All we knew is she gravitated to the eel farm when she ran away, and she smelled of a rotting eel when we got her back.

I say that was the better of the two smells because the other smell originated from something far worse. In Okinawa at that time, benjo ditches were used by the populace. They were open sewers that accepted direct deposits. Tinker would smell and look like she had swum in them.

My poor dad was the victim of all this. He had a soft spot in his heart for dogs and for his kids who loved this "dumb dog." If it were not for us, perhaps he would have never looked for her when she ran away. He was the one who had to clean matted eel slime and benjo ditch off of her. He was amazing. He kept cans of tomato juice on hand for the times he would have to do battle with that stinky dog. I never heard my dad cuss, but we did hear plenty of "dumb dog" and "stupid dog" repeated throughout the process. If there was ever a picture of an abomination, it would be benjo Tinker.

What can dads and moms bring into the home to corrupt it as detestable as eel scum and benjo stench?

- Cable channels we call art today would have gotten someone arrested for felony pornography possession just a few decades ago by a secular court.
- What business have we bringing the eel smell of parents calling people "idiots" or "I hate that person"?
- Gossip is an underrated sin by Christians, but its destructive forces are hated by God.
- Verbally tearing down a spouse, especially in the presence of the kids that need to see parents honor each other.

How much eel and benjo are we letting walk through our front door and how much eel slime are we letting sit in our living rooms? What happens when we carry the smell of this world into our homes? What if we have grown so used to the smell we no longer realize we are bringing it home at all? Maybe our house smells, and we don't even know it.

Father, please open my eyes to the sewage of this world and make us aware of its foul smell. Don't let me bring anything foul into my home. May my speech, music, movies, television, and anything else I bring with me into the home glorify You.

As a dog returns to his own vomit,
So a fool repeats his folly.
(Proverbs 26:11)

John Owen was a well-known Christian leader in the 1600s, and his book, Mortification of Sin in Believers is a classic on the subject of sin.

John Owen addressed how the horror of sin can be lost when he said, "The custom of sinning takes away the sense of it, the course of the world takes away the shame of it."[4]

The world will always minimize the gross nature and shame of sin.

-6-

THROW UP

I could never in one lifetime unweave all the fabric of imagery used to teach us God's personality. Jesus taught in parables throughout His ministry, and they have spoken deeply to the hearts of His children ever since. Some people may struggle with parables and imagery making connections, but when it comes to Scripture, just trying to understand a passage will leave the reader blessed.

So it goes with a not-so-pleasant image that many of us have seen—a dog and his vomit. God put an image involving vomit in scripture for a very good reason.

Most of us dog owners have unfortunately seen this more than a few times with our dogs. Not pleasant. Not pleasant to write about. God is using what our dogs do with the vomit to gross us out with the image of the vomit going back in.

Think about the sins you have revisited time and time again. Perhaps a life struggle of temptation with a certain sin. I thank my dogs for their gross vomit because I don't tend to think of my folly or my sin as all that vomitous. I think to myself, "I am a good guy, and everyone has struggled with this or that sin." I have seen sin so many times it isn't that gross. I don't like it, but I may not be that grossed out with it.

However, it is vomit. It's worse than vomit. I need word pictures like this to get me back on my knees praying to have eyes to see sin for what it is. Gross. Disgusting. Horrid coming out, and even more horrid should I be fool enough to return to it.

When God uses harsh imagery, we need to thank Him and realize He is communicating it is something harsh, gross, and terrible. When God had a prophet take a prostitute as a wife who then further prostituted herself after the marriage, that is what His people were doing to His love for them. Trampling and rejecting it. Truly behavior that would merit the vomit mantle.

We need God to help us recognize the full ugliness of our sins. A dog returning to its vomit is a perfect image for us. The correct sin-hating heart will help lead us to repentance and a grace replenishment straight from the throne of grace.

Father, let Your children see sin for as dark and horrid as what it is. Let us not gloss it over or frame a sin as an unfortunate mistake. Let us also recognize that when we repeat sins, we are not appreciating the horror of that sin. Show us the disgusting nature of our sins so that our desire to kill that sin in our lives will grow.

Let the word of Christ dwell in you richly in all wisdom,
teaching and admonishing one another in psalms and hymns
and spiritual songs, singing with grace in your hearts
to the Lord. (Colossians 3:16)

"The more you read the Bible;
and the more you meditate on it,
the more you will be astonished with it."
— Charles Spurgeon[5]

I Am Watching and Listening

K yle watches and listens. Our dogs are taking in a lot of things we don't give them credit for noticing. They see and hear things and associate subtle sights and sounds with real meaning. I have always wondered why Pavlov earned a place in psychology history with his salivating dogs when every dog owner knows dogs are clever and connect things rather quickly.

The closet door in our entryway has a slight hinge sound. Kyle can be lying on the back porch and hear that door open. During certain times of the day, he does not react. In the evening after dinner, however, if I open the door, Kyle will come running to the screen door. The closet door opening means I am getting my walking shoes and he is in for the most important time of the day where he gets to experience the fullness of being a dog with me, off-leash, with animals, and smelling all sorts of things.

Our close family members have an app on their phones that lets them all know where each other is at; like a George Orwell family thing. When someone comes within a few hundred yards of their house, the app makes a sound we call a "doodaloop." Their lab, Jersey, doesn't know what an app is or even a cell phone, but she has put together that sound with the fact there is a high probability a family member will be arriving in about two minutes. I think Jersey one-upped all of Pavlov's dogs.

All my dogs (except Tinker) really monitored our movements and activities. If I was in my bedroom, Kyle would be outside the door leading out to the patio. If I then walked into the living area, he would move to the patio door for that room. He was never comfortable with any barrier, including a screen door, between us. If there was no barrier, he didn't mind being away from me. However, if the screen door was closed, he would be right on the other side.

This is a picture of a faithful Bible reader. Reading the Bible is our way to monitor the personality of God. A faithful Bible reader gets uncomfortable if too far removed from God and learning about His personality. The better we know God, the better we recognize His "engine sound."

When we are listening to and watching God, like our dogs listen and watch us, we too can pick up on things. Jersey mysteriously makes a connection of a "doodaloop" to a person arriving home, God miraculously puts in us through scripture and prayer connections we could not make from our own sinful instincts.

When we are at work and we hear someone slandered, rather than remain silent, we stand up for that person. We heard the squeak of the closet door and reacted. We have watched and listened to the Father multiple times, and made the connection between an activity God hates, and how we should react.

Perhaps a friend suggests you take advantage of a merchant or a business in some way. "Everyone does it. No one will notice. Companies can take the hit." Then you hear the "doodaloop." It tells you something is not quite right. You remember God's ways from the Bible where He expects the utmost in integrity from not just business owners but from consumers. So, you point out the flaw in the suggestion and move in a way that glorifies your Father.

That is watching, listening, and putting this sound together with that activity because you have been watching and listening to God through Scripture and the Holy Spirit.

Father, let us watch and listen to You through Your Word. Let us pick up the faintest of sounds and see the smallest of details so we can see where You are moving, what You like, and how You communicate. Let us be imitators of Christ.

"Take heed and beware of covetousness,
for one's life does not consist in
the abundance of the things he possesses."
(Luke 12:15)

"Nothing teaches us about the preciousness of the Creator as
much as when we learn the emptiness of everything else."
— Charles Spurgeon[6]

WHAT WAS I THINKING?

I have to sneak in another dog here. Tag. Tag is my brother's dog, but I have spent many hours with her. We have bonded, so I am her "funcle." She is a three-quarter lab and one-quarter boxer. She turned out beautiful, and very good-natured. I love this mix.

Tag lives for all the things a normal dog should live to do. Fetch, tug-o-war, sleeping, cuddling, and then going back through the list. Gophers used to be on that list. Perhaps at the top. Until one day, after countless hours of sniffing at one gopher hole to another and exhausting herself digging them up, something amazing happened. She finally saw one.

So let me back up. Tag is not the bravest dog in the world. When I took her out to pee at my brother's cabin one night, I could not get her off the deck. Why won't she go pee? Just go! That is when I learned that she won't leave the deck unless you get a flashlight and light up the area. She is afraid of the dark. Tag is a great watchdog and can play the part, but she is not going to win any bravery medals.

Now, back to her seeing a gopher for the first time. My brother and Tag were just standing there among gopher hole wasteland when all of a sudden a gopher just popped up out of the ground and looked at Tag. Tag looked at the gopher. Tag looked at my brother, then back at the gopher, and then back at my brother. My brother could only describe the look on Tag's face as "Bluh!" She was grossed out and backed away.

Tag has never dug or sniffed at a gopher hole since. She has no interest in them, outside of peeing on their mounds occasionally. She was disgusted with the thing. After all that time, she went from dogged pursuit to total disgust.

I think we can relate a little if we look around our house, garage, or the room we are in now.

How far do you have to look to find a possession
you were so excited about on the day it arrived?
It could be clothing if that is your thing.
Is it your car?
However, the excitement wore off, didn't it?

For some strange reason, I have my old Casio PDA in a drawer in my garage. Many reading this now are like "PDA? Public Display of Affection? What are you talking about?" Well, before cell phones, cool people like me carried a "Personal Digital Assistant." You could pull it out of your pocket, read a phone number from it, put a coin in a pay phone, and call someone. It was so cool I could even write notes to myself on it. Now, I look at it and say "Bluh!" I was so proud of that thing. No one else around me had one and I spent time telling people how cool it was. It was handy, but not something that warranted any excitement now that I look back.

I heard a sermon many years ago where the pastor said one of the best sermons he could give on materialism would be to take his congregation on a field trip to a junkyard. Looking at all that junk that at one time had people so excited.

Look at that crushed Cadillac. Look at that crushed Mercedes. Look at that stereo. "Bluh." Once you see "stuff" for what it is and compare it to the eternally valuable, it changes your life.

Running from one gopher hole to the next doesn't sound like such a good idea.

Father, help me see what is valuable and what is not. Let me spend my pursuits doggedly chasing what matters and walking past that which is meaningless.

*And do not fear those who kill the body
but cannot kill the soul. But rather fear Him
who is able to destroy both soul and body in hell.*
(Jesus in Matthew 10:28)

"If you believe in a God who controls the big things, you
have to believe in a God who controls the little things. It is
we, of course, to whom things look 'little' or 'big'."
— Elisabeth Elliot[7]

-9-

Big Dogs and Small Dogs

Don't sweat the small stuff. Jesus was helpful in differentiating for us the small stuff from the big stuff in Matthew 10:28. Kyle has a sermon on this topic, and he often repeats it during our walks.

When I walk Kyle, eighty-five pounds of Rottweiler and Border Collie, it is amazing how many times little dogs run off their property in attack mode. Seeing this, you might reasonably anticipate Kyle popping them into his mouth like so many hors d'oeuvres. Not only does that not happen, but Kyle literally shows no interest. He looks at me and pulls on his leash as if to say, "Why are we even stopping for this? I don't care, why should you?"

Kyle is so dismissive I almost feel sorry for these little dogs. What an insult to be in attack mode and have your enemy not even acknowledge you.

Kyle's reaction to big dogs is quite different. Full attention. Body turns. Focused like a laser beam. Hair up at any sign of aggression. Muscles taut. Guttural low growl when the other dog doesn't act quite so friendly. Kyle knows when to go into battle mode, friend mode, or ignore mode.

Do you have little dogs and big dogs straight in your life?

Christians often confuse them. I know I do. People can look and sound scary, but Jesus is telling us they are the small dogs. People can be unspeakably cruel. World history is full of murder. The communists are estimated to have murdered up to one hundred million people in the last century. Their prisons were literally torture chambers and/or work-to-death camps.

I had a man working in my home with an accent I could not identify readily. I asked him where he grew up, and he shared it was Romania. I mentioned to him I had just watched the amazing movie, *Tortured for Christ*, which told the story of a Romanian pastor imprisoned and tortured for many years for his faith. This pastor, Richard Wurmbrand, felt the fury of man. The worker in my home knew much about Wurmbrand and said many viewed him as the Apostle Paul of Europe.

The man sadly said he believes the Church in free Romania today is not nearly as strong as it was when it had to meet in secret and were beaten and murdered if discovered. People in comfort were deceived, but people in physical danger were enlightened.

What can we learn from that?

When you feel insecure about your job or the future, do your muscles tighten?

When the wrong person wins the election do you growl?

If you hear that someone insulted you behind your back, does pride spin you around?

These are the little dogs Kyle insults and ignores. His short sermon says, "Oh, look. An angry little dog. Well, come on, let's keep going."

Jesus knew men would torture and kill Him, and He certainly felt the pain of that horror before and during His crucifixion. However, Jesus was still able to focus His attention on what was important throughout. Hebrews 12:2 says, "who for the joy that was set before Him endured the cross...."

Your big dog is the deceit that can lead a Christian into sin.

For a non-Christian, it is to hear the horrible words from God *"I never knew you."* Growl. Get your fur up. Tense your muscles.

If you do not know Christ, then meet Him. Don't be deceived. You really do need Him, and it is time to fight your pride and the lie of self-sufficiency.

If you are a Christian, Satan is still looking to deceive and rob you of your joy and the treasures that can be yours in Heaven. Tense your muscles. Give temptation a guttural growl and hate sin. Take the directives for Christians seriously, and really follow them.

Now that we can correctly identify the big dog, we can draw upon the Bible to learn how to do battle and win...which ultimately comes down to letting Christ's victory over sin do the fighting for us through truth, righteousness, the good news of the cross, faith, the joy of our salvation, the Bible, and prayer (see Ephesians 6:11-17).

Father, please help us focus our prayers and effort on the real battles that need to be fought. Let us ignore the unimportant and not invest emotion and time in areas that You would not want us to give a second thought.

"Blessed are you who weep now, For you shall laugh." (Jesus in Luke 6:21)

Every good gift and every perfect gift is from above, and comes down from the Father of lights, with whom there is no variation or shadow of turning. (James 1:17)

"Laughter is the most beautiful and beneficial therapy God ever granted humanity."
— Chuck Swindoll[8]

-10-

ALL GOOD THINGS

F un can be a scary word. It can trivialize the depth of importance of God and His will. Fun is so often associated with the world and the worthless gods so many people pursue. However, if all good things come from above, then it may be worthwhile to meditate on fun and define when it may qualify as a good thing from above. Josi and Dusty may help here.

I would take Josi and Dusty to the woods across the street daily. One particularly hot day, they chased a ground squirrel into a hole. They proceeded to dig and dig. Several clouds of dust later, all one could see was a black and a brown rear end, each with tails wagging. As many dog owners know, a tired dog is a good dog, and we were going to have *great* dogs that night.

Occasionally, one would back out and look at me panting with a raccoon ring of dust around her eyes. As I sat wondering when they would ever give up, four feet from the crater they had dug, the head of the squirrel popped up from an adjacent hole.

The squirrel surveyed the two rear ends, casually left the hole, and bounded into the woods. That was funny!

I suppose I could have deeply pondered and even wept at the brokenness of this world where the lion does *not yet* lie with the lamb. There is a right place for that mourning, but in this broken world on this day, I got a laugh. It was simply funny. I cannot always rely on my heart to identify whether laughter is a correct response, but God has endorsed laughter. If we can be wise enough to glorify God as the provider of all appropriate laughter, a mere momentary escape can be moved into an appreciation for our God who loves us enough to give us laughter.

Josi and Dusty were actors in a funny play that day, and I believe God gave me a gift. A silly memory I smile about to this day. If I choose to glorify Him with a thank you and a humble nod, I take it beyond the fun to its deeper meaning.

This meaning occurs when I remember I can laugh and really mean it because I have been redeemed by a Savior on the cross who allows me to take fun and funny beyond a momentary escape.

So, the next time you are laughing with old friends at a wedding party about "that time when" or just smiling at your pet doing that silly thing that makes you laugh, stop and glorify Jesus with a "thank you" and an acknowledgment that your laughs are deeper, richer, and more lasting only because of Him. There is no more lingering ghost of eternal death to keep our fun only at the level of momentary escape from a dreadful future.

Thank You, Father, for every gift of real fun You have given me. I know any laughter on my part would be hollow if it were not for the hope of the cross. No joke, music, performance, or time with another can have any real depth without the hope You have given me.

We love Him because He first loved us.
(1 John 4:19)

"God made the first move...He loved us before we ever loved Him (1 John 4:19), and His love is so great that Jesus willingly died for us while we were still wicked, ungodly enemies of His (Romans 5:6-10), but that is because "God, being rich in mercy, because of the great love with which he loved us, even when we were dead in our trespasses, made us alive together with Christ—by grace you have been saved" (Ephesians 2:4-5)."[9]

KYLE LOVES ME BECAUSE I LOVE HIM

W hy doesn't Kyle attack me and viciously tear me to shreds? He can. There is a huge raccoon buried in my backyard that can attest to that. Canines can be ferocious and if you have never seen that side of dogs, consider yourself fortunate.

A prophecy about Jesus on the cross reads

> *"For dogs have surrounded Me; The congrega-*
> *tion of the wicked has enclosed Me. They pierced*
> *My hands and My feet; I can count all My bones.*
> *They look and stare at Me. They divide My gar-*
> *ments among them, And for My clothing they*
> *cast lots. But You, O LORD, do not be far from*
> *Me; O My Strength, hasten to help Me! Deliver*
> *Me from the sword, My precious life from the*
> *power of the dog.* (Psalm 22:16-20)

We equate dogs with love, sloppy licks, and wagging tails, not circling fangs. We also may have a picture of wild, undo-mesticated dogs, wolves, or hyenas taking down game from a documentary. We have to look away and pity the grass-eating animal being eaten by carnivores. That is what makes this sad word picture work so horribly well.

My wife and I stopped the natural process of Kyle becoming what he might have been naturally. If raised in the wild, who is to say what Kyle would do to me if I was an unarmed, lost hiker, and his pack was hungry? The day we responded to the Craigslist ad and picked Kyle up, we started him on a course where humans were not to be bitten, feared, and not a source of food.

If I didn't receive God's love first, my maniacal desire for self-exaltation would never have been challenged. I may not have said out loud, "better to be a ruler in hell, than bow down in Heaven," but I might have lived it. Although this utter stupidity is still present in my flesh, it would rule me if God did not first show me His love. It is His revelation of love for me that brings me to my knees today.

I revealed our love for Kyle when:
I held out my hand and he fell asleep in it.
I gave him companionship and maintained it.
When I comforted him when he whined.
When I fed him and played with him.
When I took him for walks and swims.

He sees my love for him because I have manifested it. He clearly loves me, would never hurt me, and I believe he would die for me.

In the right circumstances, he could have been raised wild. He could be one of the dogs to encompass me snarling and ready to tear my flesh. That was his canine nature. However, it was my love for him that intervened, and it was God's love for me that intervened.

When I think of His love, I can see that snarling nature start to fade. Sin begins to look so bad and loyalty to my Savior looks so good. He manifested Himself to me, and I want to be near Him. I want to be in His backyard. I want Him to feed me. I want Him to tell me where we are going. I want Him to give me a job to do, like protect the sheep. I want Him to pat my head when I approach Him and hear "atta boy" because I love to please Him and hate failing Him. Why? All because He loved me first.

Father, please never let me forget that any good that has happened to me and any good there is in me is because of Your amazing grace. Thank You for loving me before I was even born and manifesting that love through the cross.

Pray, too, that we will be rescued from
wicked and evil people, for not everyone is a believer.
But the Lord is faithful; he will strengthen you
and guard you from the evil one.
(2 Thessalonians 3:3-4)

" If the Lord be with us, we have no cause of fear. His eye is
upon us, His arm over us, His ear open to our prayer - His
grace sufficient, His promise unchangeable."
— John Newton [10]

-12-

One Less Racoon

I don't think I will ever get another dog with any Rottweiler blood. They take protection a little too seriously. I heard a joke about a person's dog being the type that burglars fear most—the type they trip over in the night. Somewhere between that dog and Kyle is the perfect watchdog.

We slept with our door to the backyard completely open when Kyle was at our doorway. There was no doubt anything that entered or came near our backyard was going to be addressed. That includes raccoons.

Three times Kyle mixed it up with raccoons in our backyard and wore a scar on his snout as evidence. However, the first two times he reluctantly obeyed me and drew back to let the raccoons live out another furry, foraging day. Kyle no doubt wanted to please me in every way, but he could not contain himself with the third masked invader.

The third raccoon, may he rest in peace, did not make it. I could not prevent Kyle from working his way up from the underbelly to the neck.

Kyle was ferocious during all this.

If I am ever confronted by an armed man who wishes to do me wrong, I feel sorry for him. I hope I don't die at the hands of a violent person, but if I do, I hope I am able to warn him. I want to at least be able to explain the great peril he is in. God loves me a lot. If someone harms me and then goes on to die without the cleansing blood of our Savior applied, then I sense the raccoon will have a much better eternal fate.

We know from a global perspective of Scripture God is not promising His children will never experience violence. History has shown us frequently the opposite since the time of the murders of the Apostles themselves. However, I do know Christians are protected from the dangers that matter, and God stands as a better protector from true harm than Kyle.

This world is not full of perfect people. Some are downright wicked. However, we know we have the ultimate Kyle lying at the door of our very heart guarding us against the one that can do us true harm.

I do not fear physically with Kyle at my door. And I need not fear spiritually with a great God who loves me protecting my very soul.

John Newton, even with his memories of being a slave ship captain understood, *"If the Lord be with us, we have no cause of fear. His eye is upon us, His arm over us, His ear open to our prayer - His grace sufficient, His promise unchangeable."* He went from a wretched slave trader to a strong force behind the move to end slavery. He could have let his past beat him to a useless pulp, but he understood that his God was guarding him and was not tossing him overboard.

Father, I have my fears. I can't deny them. Many of them are irrational. Some are based on my pride more than anything. Thank You for guarding my heart and taking me through this life to its very end. You are an awesome God and faithful protector.

You shall have no other gods before me.
(Deuteronomy 5:7)

"Paul's exhortation to do everything for the glory of God is more than pious idealism. It is an integral part of the sacred revelation and is to be accepted as the very Word of Truth. It opens before us the possibility of making every act of our lives contribute to the glory of God. Lest we should be too timid to include everything, Paul mentions specifically eating and drinking. This humble privilege we share with the beasts that perish. If these lowly animal acts can be so performed as to honor God, then it becomes difficult to conceive of one that cannot."
— A.W. Tozer[11]

DOG SPELLED BACKWARDS IS GOD

People have noted that "dog spelled backward is god." These folks are probably dog enthusiasts and probably meant it in appreciation for all the fun things God has put into our canine friends. However, the little pithy saying may contain a warning for us all.

God's commandments deserve a slow read and meditation. First, let's acknowledge there is only one God, one Creator, and one Savior. Yet, God is acknowledging the presence or reality of these "small g" gods we invent.

No review of dogs and how they might inspire us toward a deeper understanding of God would be complete without considering whether we need to hear "you should have no dogs before me." God has revealed many ugly truths to me. Mostly about myself. The older I get, the more I see the tentacles of my sinful nature and my fleshly aversion to turning to God.

What do we do when we need clear, cool water on a hot day? God told His people in Isaiah 12:3, "Therefore with joy you will draw water from the wells of salvation." Many years later, Jesus told a woman He was the "living water" she really needed. This world is a hot day. Christians admit their sinful nature and know that something has gone horribly wrong with this world.

Our flesh does not want to thank and appreciate the gracious giver. What we should do is in all our ways acknowledge God and glorify Him. When asked whether God was a megalomanic since He wants so much glory. John Piper said in part:

"God created humans so that they will worship him. That's true. That's absolutely true... Every pleasure that isn't rooted in God will fail you. Your heart was made to find greatest and longest happiness in God. ...If sin keeps you from supreme joy in God, sin needs to go, not God.."[12]

A dog lover so enjoys dogs, it is very easy to come home from a horrible day, spiritually convicted, tired, or stressed, and reach first for our dog, not our God. We should be praising God for our day. I know I reach for things other than God.

Television, food, a person, and yes, even my Kyle can be a diversion. Dogs are infectious. They are normally happy. Their wagging tails and excitement toward us can be the ultimate compliment. It is easy to play with your pup and not once think of the Creator of the puppy.

Christians need to be sensitive that at any given moment we are susceptible to reaching for satisfaction outside of God.

When we reach for our dog or start out the door with them for their walk, we are better aligning ourselves with God if we start with a prayer acknowledging God's glory and worth and a grateful heart for our dogs (or any good thing). Our dogs are a glorification of God's creativity and awesomeness, not a replacement for glorifying Him and enjoying Him.

Father, thank You so much for the many things in our creation that bring us smiles. A beautiful sunset, coffee with a good friend, a lush park to walk in, and a funny dog. Help us never reach for any of these good things to replace You. May we rather use them to increase our enjoyment and appreciation of You, our amazing God.

Then a loud wail will rise throughout the land of Egypt,
a wail like no one has heard before or will ever hear again.
But among the Israelites it will be so peaceful that not even a
dog will bark. Then you will know that the LORD makes a
distinction between the Egyptians and the Israelites.
(Exodus 11:6-7 NLT)

"The Blood of Jesus washes away our past and the
Name of Jesus opens up our future."
— Jesse Duplantis[13]

Not a Dog Shall Bark

I s your dog a good watchdog? Does your dog have ears that can be downright frightening in the ability to perceive sounds? Here are some common themes you have probably noticed about your dog that the rest of us has noticed as well:

- Your dog knows each engine that regularly arrives at your home.
- Your dog can hear a car it recognizes long before you ever hear it.
- Your dog can detect very slight variations in a voice and sense something is wrong.
- Your dog can flip itself onto its feet from a deep sleep from a sound you didn't hear while wide awake (at least when it was young).

Imagine the greatest upheaval in your community that you have ever witnessed and seeing your dog sleep through it. Sound improbable? Of course, it is improbable.

But...

Exodus tells the story of the final act God took to free His enslaved people from the Egyptian pharaoh. It was catastrophic. Every firstborn male who lived in a home that was not sealed in the blood of the Passover lamb was to die. God warned in Exodus 11:6-7.

Picture your dog sleeping through this night. Then ask yourself, why did God mention dogs at all here? If any creature were to hear this awful night as families shrieked at the death of the sons, brothers, husbands, uncles, friends, and grandfathers, it would be a dog. They would be howling and on alert.

Could it be that God is using dogs to tell us something deeper? That not only does the blood of Christ over the door posts of our hearts seal us and protect us from death, but that death should not even have the power to disturb us like it once had. If it does disturb and frighten us, perhaps that is because our faith and understanding are not what they should be. However, we have no cause for alarm. Dogs did not need to rise up and warn God's children in the night.

This is a strong picture. Those of us in Christ are safe. Sealed. Delivered.

The Angel of Death can harvest our bones and the bones of our neighbors, but we are eternally alive and well with Jesus. Egypt (the enslavement to sin) cannot have power over us. Perhaps, that is why God was so careful to include this unique detail in this account.

The world may rage on with horrible things ultimately happening to those who have not been sealed by the blood of the Lamb, but among those in Christ, we do not even need our watchdogs to disturb us.

Father, please show me the fullness of the power of Your salvation. May Your saving grace embolden me to sleep through matters that have no power over me. Don't let me even stir at things You have already promised cannot hurt me.

Yet they did not obey or incline their ear,
but followed the counsels and the dictates
of their evil hearts,
and went backward and not forward.
(Jeremiah 7:24)

-15-

Poor Soldier

It was time to leave Okinawa, the only place I knew. I was almost nine. I had never watched Scooby Doo or eaten at a Taco Bell, but I was excited at all the stories of life in the United States. I would have stayed in Okinawa the rest of my life if it meant leaving Tinker. My dad and mom knew our attachment and were willing to pay Tinker's way back stateside. That was no small ordeal. It was very expensive and complicated. We had to board her on a military base in a kennel that was part of a military canine training facility. My brother and I visited her during those weeks when we had no house and were awaiting our flight home.

We were able to take her out of the kennel and bring her right into a fenced training ground with a huge canine obstacle course. As soon as she checked the wide exterior fencing and decided she could not escape, she came back to us and played ball. She loved to play fetch and make popping sounds with tennis balls.

We were approached by a young soldier. The poor fella should have just kept walking, but he lingered with us and enjoyed watching us play with our dog. He was a K-9 handler.

We told him how difficult and untrainable Tinker was. He told us, "All dogs can be trained." He explained we just needed to know how, and then asked if we wanted him to show us. My brother and I agreed, but we were not as confident in believing an adult as kids usually are.

With the military lead and the choke chain around Tinker's neck, the "training" commenced. It went on for a while. I most remember the "wall." There was a successive row of walls. The first wall was about one foot high, and the last one looked like a mountain. I remember that poor man standing at the one-foot wall trying to drag Tinker over it. She could have stepped over it, but she would not. She preferred to sit on her side, paws dug in, choking. She would have suffocated before going over that wall. He brought Tinker back in utter disgust and said she was the stupidest dog he had ever seen. He walked away quite irritated. She was the smartest dog I have ever known.

Jeremiah and other prophets were sent to warn God's people to turn from their evil ways. They were ignored and sometimes killed.

What causes people to opt for asphyxiation rather than stepping over a foot-high board?

What causes Christians to hear the leading of the Holy Spirit and ignore it?

"I won't go to pastoral counseling with my spouse because it's not my problem"...gasp..."I like those cable stations, and I don't stumble that often"...choke. "I don't think my drinking is a problem really"...gag.

We may have come far from where we started as a Christian, but there is another wall that may seem unattractive or formidable. Maybe the walls are getting taller as God takes us through the course. However, our handler knows our capabilities and will not lead us to tackle something we can't get beat with His help. Looking back at how far God has taken us can keep us from digging in our heals and proceeding in faith.

Pray:

Father, which one-foot wall am I refusing to step over? How is my stubbornness dishonoring You and hurting me and the ones I love? Break me, Father. Break my heart so I see it and respond to the leading of Your Spirit.

"You have heard that it was said, 'You shall love your neighbor and hate your enemy.' But I say to you, love your enemies, bless those who curse you, do good to those who hate you, and pray for those who spitefully use you and persecute you, that you may be sons of your Father in heaven; for He makes His sun rise on the evil and on the good, and sends rain on the just and on the unjust. For if you love those who love you, what reward have you? Do not even the tax collectors do the same? And if you greet your brethren only, what do you do more than others? Do not even the tax collectors do so? Therefore you shall be perfect, just as your Father in heaven is perfect.
— Jesus in Matthew 5:43-48

-16-

So Forgiving

Have you ever hurt your dog by accident? I have. It's awful. Perhaps the only being in your life that would never do anything to hurt you out of spite or anger or irritation is your dog. There are, of course, some bad dogs out there that for whatever reason turn on their owners, but for the most part, that does not describe most of our loving pets.

I was climbing way up in a tree using a bow saw to cut limbs. Josi and Dusty were below. I was not cutting big limbs, so even if they fell I was not concerned about them getting hurt. They would probably jump out of the way anyway. What I hadn't accounted for was slipping and having my saw fly out of my hand, which is exactly what happened. The saw did not drop harmlessly to the ground.

What were the chances? That saw hit my Dusty square on the snout. Not just the handle, but the blade part. It hurt. Nothing beyond first aid was needed, fortunately, but I felt like dirt. I told her I was sorry repeatedly and gave her all sorts of attention for a good long while. However, she wore that little scar for the rest of her life.

You would think that our relationship would be scarred for the rest of her life, too, but it wasn't. Our relationship wasn't scarred, as far as I could tell, for any perceivable time. No growl. No silent treatment. No leaving my side. I was negligent and wrong, but the forgiveness was immediate. Dusty must have fully embraced what the Apostle Paul said in Romans 12:17, "Repay no one evil for evil. Have regard for good things in the sight of all men." He didn't give me the bite or even the scowl I deserved.

While confronting people who drop saws on us may not be wrong, we are to forgive them, too. There is room for debate on points of Scripture, but I don't see a lot of room for that on the issue of forgiveness. We have a pretty clear idea of what God expects. Our forgiveness is to be deep, and certainly at least as forgiving as a dog.

Pray*:*

Jesus, Your vision of forgiveness was radical in its time, and it is radical now in our culture. Please help us to radically pursue You by imitating Your love and forgiveness, even to the point where we would pray for those who crucify us.

But if the Spirit of Him who raised Jesus from the dead dwells in you, He who raised Christ from the dead will also give life to your mortal bodies through His Spirit who dwells in you. Therefore, brethren, we are debtors—not to the flesh, to live according to the flesh. For if you live according to the flesh you will die; but if by the Spirit you put to death the deeds of the body, you will live. For as many as are led by the Spirit of God, these are sons of God."
(Romans 8:11-14)

17

LEAD ME ON

Hume Lake, nestled in the mountains of the Kings Canyon area is gorgeous. It contains a fantastic Christian camp environment. Surrounded by flowing crystal clear rivers, waterfalls, massive sequoia trees, and fun campgrounds, it is also known for bears. Largely they are peaceful and walk about the camp and cabins at night foraging for whatever may have been dropped on the ground.

We visited this area often. My wife and I had a small truck with a shell and no kids at the time, so taking Josi and Dusty was not difficult. They were in heaven swimming in the lake and hiking with us. They slept great at night after having been pooped out from all the running each day.

One evening, we took them to a meadow we knew would be full of bears when it got dark. Bears congregated in this meadow waiting for all the campers to go to sleep so they could walk the camp. They laid there in peace and flattened the tall grass each night.

Josi and Dusty had never seen a bear. They were aware of coyotes, but not bears, so we decided to take them out to the meadow early while it was still open to humans. What we saw was amazing. The moment Josi and Dusty hit the flattened grass and smelled the strong scents, they got down low. They didn't lie down exactly, but their chests were about an inch from the ground, and they were looking around at everything.

It was so obvious their instincts were telling them something very large and powerful and dangerous could be nearby. My wife and I had never seen them react that way to anything before or since. Phenomenal how animals just know.

However, human instinct is not as trustworthy. Jude 1:3-10 cautions us about those who think like a beast:

> *Beloved, while I was very diligent to write to you concerning our common salvation, I found it necessary to write to you exhorting you to contend earnestly for the faith which was once for all delivered to the saints.*
>
> *For certain men have crept in unnoticed, who long ago were marked out for this condemnation, ungodly men, who turn the grace of our God into lewdness and deny the only Lord God and our Lord Jesus Christ....But these speak evil of whatever they do not know; and whatever they know naturally, like brute beasts, in these things they corrupt themselves.*

This natural instinct of the unsaved is one that cannot be trusted because it originates from ignorance. Let's now look at a supernatural, "de-animalized" guiding force that Paul speaks of in Romans 8:11-14.

We see there are animal-like, unthinking instincts, and sinful natures present in this world. There is also something called "the power of the Spirit" and being "led by the Spirit." One force is bad, one force is good. Both are bigger than we are. Our sinful nature is powerful and beyond our understanding, but so is the leading of the Spirit of God.

I need the Spirit-led life because my instincts don't sense danger from spiritual bears on my own. I need the Spirit to alert me to those bears because my instinct is to ignore the smells of evil.

Pray*:*

Lord, I am without the tools to detect and conquer evil on my own. I need Your Spirit to lead me in the paths I should walk. Only You can save me and guide me correctly. I am powerless in this area. Thank You for already showing me so much, but I want more so I can imitate Christ and be the image of You that I should be.

For I fear lest, when I come, I shall not find you such as I wish,
and that I shall be found by you such as you do not wish;
lest there be contentions, jealousies, outbursts of wrath, selfish
*ambitions, **backbitings**, whisperings, conceits, tumults;*
— Apostle Paul
(2 Corinthians 12:20 KJV emphasis added)

18

NOW THAT'S HOW YOU BACKBITE

Tinker was truly vicious when she wanted to be. Multiple times when she got away from us, we have seen her attack another domesticated dog in really a frightening display of aggression. How embarrassed we were when it happened.

We never saw her actually hurt the other dog, but it was scary to watch and more frightening to hear. The other dog, often larger, inevitably wound up on the ground in a submissive posture, feet up, neck bared.

You could almost hear the other dog say, "I get it. You are not really a dog. You're a freak. Just don't kill me."

There was this one time we did not see her dominate. Tinker got out of the front door of our hilltop home in Okinawa multiple times. One time, it was not hard to get her back. In fact, it was the only time she ever came back on her own, and she came back very quickly.

There was a very large dog that lived down the street. Maybe three times the size of Tinker. Tinker did not like this dog. Dogs are funny on walks.

At one house, the dog we pass is no big deal, and then in another, there is doggie hatred. Somewhere, there are written rules we don't have access to that tells dogs when to despise each other. This large dog, Tinker hated.

That day when Tinker gained her freedom, she went one house over and turned down the street where this dog lived. My dad followed curious to see where Tinker was headed. My dad saw that very large dog was outside walking around but did not see Tinker.

Tinker crept up on that dog silently and literally bit him hard on the back. The dog had no idea what had happened. Before any fight could occur, Tinker turned and ran back home as fast as she could (and she was a lightning streak). She beat my dad to our front door, barked, scratched, and was let in. The first and last time she ever came home voluntarily. My sister said she had never heard Tinker make the sounds she made as she was running from that dog.

Backbiting is mentioned in 2 Corinthians 12:20 by Paul to describe unprovoked defamation without giving a person a chance to defend themselves.

Backbiting is one of those things we would usually deny that we do. We should not be so quick or so sure. Backbiting can be very subtle.

It is associated with passive-aggressive people, which may be most people except those with explosive tempers. Passive aggressive people don't explode. Passive aggressive people wait for the opportunity, sneak up behind people, and take painful bites. Then they run away by saying, "Oh, I was just kidding," or "Can't you take a joke." People frequently take a bite out of people who have hurt them when that person is not in the room or cannot otherwise defend him/herself.

Pray*:*

Father, if someone has hurt me or someone else, give me the courage to confront them in a noble, caring way. Please remind me to pray beforehand so I can reflect You in my words. Don't let my hurts make me into a backbiter, but rather a loving, Spirit-led confronter.

A righteous man regards the life of his animal,
but the tender mercies of the wicked are cruel.
(Proverbs 12:10)

-19-

GOD ALSO LOVES YOUR DOG

How easy it was for me to go on a walk with Kyle and smile as I pondered what a great team we made. BFFs. Well, I am leaving someone out. God was with us, too. He cared about Kyle as well. After all, He made Kyle; I didn't.

This seems like a small point, but it's not. A life in Christ means not just loving God but learning more and more about God. To know God better is to love and honor Him even more. I forget sometimes just how much He enjoys His own creation. He loves animals and He wants animals treated well.

"A righteous man regards the life of his animal." That reveals such a tender heart. Think about a God that can speak the universe into existence. He knows every atom in your body. He has raised kingdoms and taken them down. He developed a plan to save His children from themselves while "they were yet sinners." Yet, that bigger than imaginable God cares about your dog! By the way, He cares about how you treat your dog and other animals.

Did you see God's use of irony in this verse? The *"tender mercies of the wicked are cruel."* A sign of a cruel person can be how they treat animals or ignore their plight.

73

We can't individually save the world. However, if we have decided to own an animal, God expects our "tender mercies" to be real. Ask yourself if you are reasonably meeting the needs of any animals you own.

The key word to that is "reasonably." No one is expecting you to cuddle the cows in your herd, but are they getting the veterinary attention they need to prevent suffering? Kyle was almost nine and tore his ACL. That was very tough. He was near the end of his life, our funds were limited, and surgery was very expensive. The surgery did not assure he would be healed, and the surgery itself involved a long kennel time.

Faced with that decision, I opted not to provide for the surgery. I factored in that Kyle enjoyed nothing more than swimming. He could swim for hours. We lived right by the water. So, our nightly walk became his nightly swim. I was sad he could not run like he used to, but I did regard my dog and tried to act reasonably to meet his needs. I think he was happy. The beavers there hated him, but oh well.

Some people may have money problems, housing issues, and work issues and may not be able to perfectly meet their pet's needs. However, God wants us to care and do what we can.

I should add that I have known people who didn't have the wherewithal to have a hamster, let alone a dog, but they owned several dogs. Their dogs stayed in their backyard, sometimes ill-fed, and rarely loved on. (Yes, we fed them on occasion and took them on walks ourselves).

So, if you are considering a pet, make sure that your decision to get the pet is based on a regard for *"the life of the animal."*

Pray*:*

Father, let me be a good steward of the animals You have graced me with. Give me a good understanding of where my efforts to care for an animal should begin and comfort in knowing where they should end. Do not allow me to place my love for animals over people but be the blessing to those You call me to be.

We can define play as a fun, imaginative, non-compulsory, non-utilitarian activity filled with creative spontaneity and humor, which gives perspective, diversion, and rest from the necessary work of daily life. In light of God's sovereignty and faithful love, play for the Christian should demonstrate and encourage hope, delight, gratitude, and celebration... This sure hope in God's sovereign power and loving-kindness enables us to play with abandon, even before the great wedding banquet begins.
— Erik Thoennes[14] "Holy Play"

This article by Erik Thoennes entitled "Holy Play" is a worthy read on the Christian life.

-20-

You Can Go Out and Play

God made many animals that love to play. The lives of dogs are mainly devoted to it until their bodies wear out. Does it surprise anyone that dogs' bodies wear out so quickly when they cover more miles in a year than a human in a lifetime? They really live! How could the God who made otters not endorse fun?

Have you noticed how Hollywood often plays Christians and pastors as fools in their plots? It seems like that was the shift starting in the 1960s. Often the clergy were represented as rigid and frowning and religious people as stern and condemning. Laughter, play, and fun were rarely represented.

I don't think many movies would show a pastor or a Christian rolling around on the ground playing tug-o-war with their dog. After all, in the mind of so many Hollywood writers, Christians can't have fun. No Christians were once atheists. No Christians have doctoral degrees in the sciences. Christian couples are never romantic. Christians are always lurking to judge you for any cussword or glass of wine.

An easily overlooked passage in Zechariah addresses what Jerusalem would look like when God brings His chosen people back from their captivity.

> *Old men and old women shall again sit in the streets of Jerusalem, each one with his staff in his hand because of great age. The streets of the city Shall be full of boys and girls Playing in its streets.* (Zechariah 8:4-5)

Doesn't that sound like God is looking forward to people enjoying life again? Sounds to me like He enjoys listening to kids playing.

I read over those verses many times without them striking a chord. I read them as prophecy and history. I didn't read them as speaking to the *personality* of God. I now read those verses as showing me God liked to see and hear good things. Old folks being old folks, and children *playing*.

It may disappoint Hollywood writers to know we Christians play. We do all sorts of fun things and often we play with our dogs. I have every reason to believe from Scripture that play is good. It is a gift. God probably delights in a balanced life of His children and seeing and listening to me play tug of war with Kyle in the backyard. I used a rope tied to a discarded rubber boat bumper. I can swirl it around my head until Kyle tackles it before the tug of war begins.

If you have a bad back, tug-o-war using a rope is so much better than getting yanked and jerked around closer to the ground.

If you are prone to feeling guilty about play, perhaps you are a workaholic or for whatever reason, you rarely ever engage in play for other reasons.

I would guess you either don't have a dog or you have a very bored dog.

Pray:

Father, bless our playtime. Please give us the wisdom to know when play should start and when it should end. Provide us with a holy balance between work and play. Allow families to use play to bond and enjoy the deeper joy of their salvation rather than use it purely for escape. Thank You for play. Strengthen those who are in dark times of ill health or in prison or cannot now engage in play.

I have seen all the works that are done under the sun;
and indeed, all is vanity and grasping for the wind.
(Ecclesiastes 1:14)

-21-

GRASPING FOR COYOTES

O ur homes were in a larger metropolitan area, but there were still natural riverbeds and biking trails. Josi and Dusty walked in one of these riverbeds almost every night. The foliage was lush, jungle-like, and packed with coyotes. Coyotes are such resilient animals.

Josi and Dusty were interested in the coyotes, and the coyotes were interested in Josi and Dusty. It appears the coyotes knew exactly why they were interested in our dogs. Josi and Dusty were spade, so not sure expanding DNA diversity was part of their interest. It is not unheard of for coyotes to mate with domesticated dogs. I have heard coyotes can be interested in eating other dogs or they can consider dogs as trespassers and competitors to "beat up."

A scenario that would play out multiple times each month was a single coyote would emerge and get Josi and Dusty to chase it.

This worked every time. Josi and Dusty would crash through trees and brush in pursuit of a coyote. I was never too concerned for a few reasons. I figured they could take care of themselves. They were larger than coyotes and there

81

were two of them after all. Also, I was close enough that if I heard something going horribly wrong, I was prepared to crash through the jungle and rescue them.

Upon return, I would always ask the girls (like I expect an answer) if they accomplished what they set out to do. It was a joke meant for me as the sole audience because I knew they had no plan whatsoever. It was stimulus-response. Saw coyote, and chased the same. They were not protecting any sheep. They didn't want to procreate. They didn't want to eat a coyote. They were just behaving as a potential meal being lured into the pack.

A repeated thought in the wisdom literature of Ecclesiastes was that in life "...all is vanity and grasping for the wind." I can almost hear the author, in today's terms saying that so much of life is just "stimulus-response, stimulus-response."

When speaking to people open to religion in general, but doubt the need for Jesus, I usually compliment them for at least seeking meaning. It's a step in the right direction to finding Him.

Christians need to search for meaning, even though we have embraced the core of meaning, Jesus Himself. We can often go through a day and reflect on how much of what we did was "stimulus-response."

We can easily forget that each day carries meaning and opportunities to do meaningful things. While only Jesus could go through a day and score 100 percent, we don't have to score 0 percent either.

Seeing a coyote and just chasing it with no plan at all is not a good idea. Especially when the coyote may have a definite plan for us. A dog guarding sheep should chase a coyote. A dog hunting pheasant should sniff them out and point. A dog herding cattle should nip at some heels. A Christian should pursue things that glorify God and result in rewards. However, we don't have to strive after the wind or live "another day, another dollar" existence.

Pray*:*

Father, please give me the wisdom to know what to chase on this planet and when to chase it. Let me use my talents and efforts wisely and with purpose.

God will never leave us or forsake us if we are in Christ (Hebrews 13:5), but that does not mean He is promising to explain every event in our life. The Christian life is a series of tests.

22

No Reason to Panic

J osi and Dusty. The two sisters. Half lab and half Australian shepherd. Wonderful dogs. Love the memories my wife and I had with them. I miss them. Josi was the alpha of the two sisters. She attached herself firmly to me. Dusty attached herself firmly to Josi. That shouldn't surprise anyone who has read a little about dogs and packs. Dogs have hierarchies and relationships like people.

Since they were brought home as puppies, my wife and I were good dog owners. They were well fed and given a comfortable life. I can't remember any owner failures of any significance. We never gave them a reason to doubt us. However, one sad day Josi panicked, and it literally killed her. We traveled to a wedding and brought Josi and Dusty. We had a safe backyard at a relative's home where we could keep them while we were at the wedding. Good fencing all around.

We don't know exactly what happened, nor does it matter. Apparently, when Josi heard our car leave, she panicked. She must have thought we drove a few hundred miles to just leave her there.

I was the center of her world. Somehow, she managed to get out of that backyard and run. Even though we were hundreds of miles from home, she knew to run south. That meant a black dog, running south, on a busy highway at night. We lost her. We cried for days, and I am crying now writing this many years later.

King Hezekiah was a pretty decent king. He had faithfully carried out much of his work to restore his kingdom to godly practices. When attacked by overwhelming forces, he was an encouraging leader to his people and wisely turned to God for deliverance. God delivered him and his people in a mighty and miraculous way.

After he had performed well, 2 Chronicles 32:31 contains a point that may be easily overlooked. After God's deliverance from attackers, and after God healed Hezekiah of a serious illness, another powerful country sent emissaries to his land.

> *However, regarding the ambassadors of the princes of Babylon, whom they sent to him to inquire about the wonder that was done in the land, God withdrew from him, in order to test him, that He might know all that was in his heart.*

Wait! Is God allowed to withdraw? Drive away?

Maybe this is a good time to reflect on C.S. Lewis when he reminded us that while our Savior is a lion, he is not a *tame* lion.[15] He is not under our rules, or our personal paradigm of what God is supposed to do. It is also good to remember God tests the people He loves. It is mentioned throughout the Old Testament and New Testament.

There do seem to be times when God doesn't seem close at hand when we are dry and all we can do is cry because we don't know what to do.

Some people start what they think is a healthy Christian lifestyle, but they are really only focused on all the good things that come with a "Christian lifestyle." God wants our heart, not just practice. Often, our Christian lifestyle is tossed a hand grenade. Spouses leave, hurt us, or we think they hurt us. Children walk away. Jobs are lost. Cancer knocks. We relapse into a sin we thought we had overcome with our "lifestyle." Something in our heart just seems to cave for no reason we understand. Could God have withdrawn from me? Drove away?

Maybe He does withdraw in certain areas to test us. Maybe we are being tested to show we are not running on autopilot but will hang on through the thick of what we don't understand now.

> *Ask Yourself...*
> *Is the God I know from Scripture going to truly drive off and leave me in this backyard?*
> *Is that the character of a God who would hang on a cross and have all my horrible sins placed on Him?*

> *Am I lacking in faith or am I going to get*
> *through this because I know I am being tested*
> *by a great and merciful God?*
> *Have I been depending on myself or that the*
> *good times will continue until I die?*

God will never leave us or forsake us if we are in Christ (Hebrews 13:5), but that does not mean He is promising to explain every event in our life . The Christian life is a series of tests.

Pray:

Father, give me the strength to run the good race and finish this life well. Do not let me be shaken by discouragement or confusion.

Then Jesus went out from there and departed to the region of
Tyre and Sidon. And behold, a woman of Canaan came from
that region and cried out to Him, saying,
"Have mercy on me, O Lord, Son of David!
My daughter is severely demon-possessed."
But He answered her not a word. And His disciples came and
urged Him, saying, "Send her away, for she cries out after us."
But He answered and said, "I was not sent except to the lost
sheep of the house of Israel."
Then she came and worshiped Him, saying, "Lord, help me!"
But He answered and said, "It is not good to take the children's
bread and
throw it to the little dogs."
And she said, "Yes, Lord, yet even the little dogs eat the crumbs
which fall from their masters' table."
Then Jesus answered and said to her,
"O woman, great is your faith!
Let it be to you as you desire."
And her daughter was healed from that very hour.
(Matthew 15:21-28)

23

I'LL TAKE SCRAPS

The Bible uses animals to express learning points. Many Bible teachers have used illustrations from animals as well, including dogs. Jesus used dogs to powerfully communicate the promise of salvation through faith in Christ for all the world.

Jesus starts out with this woman kind of stern sounding. However, as the story unfolds, you can see He was drawing something out from her He wanted all generations to read and understand. He used a picture of a little dog begging at a table perfectly to do so. Not just a little dog begging, but a little dog getting!

The Jewish understanding of salvation was about to be rocked. So many of the Jewish religious elite looked down on non-Jews. Jesus was foreshadowing that the Gentile was soon be invited into salvation from an entirely new covenant that was not centered on the nation of Israel, sacrifices, and law but would open to the entire world. There was going to be enough of Christ's work on the cross for every nation and every generation.

The little dogs at the table will not just have scraps, but everything they could imagine and more—salvation through faith. No performance exam is to be administered prior to salvation. Begging at the right table from the right person was all that was to be required.

Did you notice the disciples in this story? Not very much compassion was there. "Just get rid of her, Jesus, she is driving us crazy," they were urging. I wonder how they treated little hungry puppies. I am not sure they would have qualified as dog lovers. Jesus quietly showed them how to love at the same time He was extending grace to a Gentile.

What must they have thought when they heard that awesome woman's answer? Did they want to crawl under a rock? Were they further irritated at Jesus? After Jesus was crucified, rose, and they really started to "get it," did they ever withhold scraps from a begging little dog? Maybe they became dog lovers.

Pray:

Thank You, Lord, that salvation is not reserved for a nationality, people of only certain skin color, or ethnicity, but to all who believe and arrive at the Master's table.

Commit your works to the LORD,
And your thoughts will be established.
(Proverbs 16:3)

24

PREPARE OR YOU'RE WASTING YOUR TIME

Have you watched nature shows of wolves, coyotes, and other animals hunting their prey? It is the same repeated dynamic. Predators move as close to their prey as possible before they begin a chase. Stealth sometimes gets them so close that all that is needed is a pounce. Even cheetahs close as much distance as possible with their dinner before they explode into the seventy-mile-an-hour run. However, even cheetahs don't always catch their prize.

Now compare your dog to what you have seen on these shows. Most often, they are pretty dismal. Somewhere in the domestication process, dogs have lost the whole point of stealth. Tinker was sneaky and I have no doubt could hunt effectively, but my other dogs were pathetic. Their idea of hunting was -see a squirrel, run fast. Never did I see them try to be quiet, get low, go slow, stay concealed, or wait patiently.

Their inability at stalking showed in their dismal results. Josi and Dusty scored exactly one squirrel catch in their life spans. They even had the advantage of hunting together. Walking along a dirt road we often traveled, there was nature on the south side of the road and some houses that backed up to the road on the north side. There were ground squirrels galore.

One day, they were on the north side by the back fences of a house. They were sniffing around casually. Apparently, the dog in that backyard heard them and ran toward the back of its property to bark at Josi and Dusty as any decent dog following the rules would do. That dog, running to the back of the property caused a squirrel to panic and run up and over the block wall.

This had the unintended consequence of the squirrel crawling down the other side of the wall one foot away from Dusty's nose. Dusty, having never had any physical contact with one of the thousands of squirrels she had pursued in her life, gently plucked it off the wall and stood there just amazed. The squirrel, in the jaws of a dog, knew exactly what to do. It bit Dusty right on the top of her snout, causing Dusty to drop it with a shriek of pain. After Josi recovered from the shock of what was going on, she ran over and was able to engage the squirrel. Although technically caught, the squirrel did end up getting away alive. The first and last Josi and Dusty squirrel they ever came close to catching.

Similar story with Kyle. On his 10,000th squirrel chase, he finally caught one that was maybe just clueless and kept overrunning his escape holes in the ground. Any squirrel caught by Kyle is just not sharp and a perfect candidate for natural selection. My wife and I weren't prepared for this. Kyle's neck muscles, being Olympian level, allowed him to throw that squirrel straight up in the air right on top of us. That squirrel easily was fifteen feet in the air, causing us to scramble in a panic to avoid the squirrel rain.

The point is my dogs wasted so much of their lives on the pursuit of squirrels that was largely hopeless. Anyone watching could see why. There was no stalking, just running. No reflection on what hadn't worked at all for years.

Proverbs 16:3 instructs to "Commit your works to the LORD, And your thoughts will be established." That is exactly what I don't do enough. I fail to commit my works to the Lord. Perhaps, I figure some works don't merit bringing to the Lord. I forget to pray about important decisions and fail to seek wise counsel. I often choose to run as fast as I can without establishing purpose and then fail to reflect on why something didn't work.

Pray:

Lord, please grace me with the wisdom not to run headlong into life. I confess I do that and know it yields poor results. Allow my mind to return to You for all my important decisions and pursuits.

"...always with all prayer and supplication in the Spirit,
being watchful to this end
with all perseverance and supplication
for all the saints—."
(Ephesians 6:18)

25

IF YOU LOVE IT, LIFT IT

Our Honey Badger, I mean, dog, Tinker, had to be watched closely. She was sneaky. Keeping her was most akin to perhaps keeping a coyote or fox as a pet. It took extra effort and some occasional apologies to the unsuspecting public or visitors. This was particularly true on one occasion I remember well.

When I was nine, we had some awesome cousins come for a visit. They stayed a few days with us, and fun memories were made. They brought a guinea pig. I liked most animals, so I thought this was a pretty cool pet and looked forward to playing with it.

We didn't think about Tinker or their Guinea pig as our family guests arrived. Basically, this was the equivalent of not thinking about smoking a cigar in a natural gas plant. As my cousin was walking through our living room with the harmless, cute Guinea pig in a small wire cage, Tinker maneuvered herself quietly next to my cousin. She was eye-level with the caged, low-in-the-food-chain animal.

Most dogs may have provided some warning by sniffing the cage, showing interest, or something that indicated we may need to be a little careful here. Not with Tinker. As soon as she was in position, she immediately sank her scary-looking fangs through the screen of the cage and latched on.

It was immediate, and she needed to be pulled away before letting go. No sniffing. No growling. Nothing a domesticated dog might have done. Sharks at least bump shark cages or swim by them a few times. Not Tinker. It was game on immediately.

We are instructed to lift up our brothers and sisters in prayer in Ephesians 6:18. 1 Peter 5:8 warns us, "Be sober, be vigilant; because your adversary the devil walks about like a roaring lion, seeking whom he may devour."

This presents a sobering challenge maybe not all Christians are up to facing. The easier part is just reading the verse and seeing we need to pray for each other. Pray for our families. Pray for our pastors. Pray for our church. Pray for our missionaries. Pray for ministries.

Where it may get difficult is admitting why we fail to pray as we should. I find it difficult because the reason is unpleasant for me to admit. I haven't cared enough. Ugh. Hard to admit and confess. I can come up with other excuses that make me feel better about myself. I mean, life is busy. I do get tired. However, I know down deep the problem is more serious than that.

Augustine too often nails me when he said long ago, "He that loveth little prayeth little, he that loveth much prayeth much."[16]

Had my cousin been warned of the danger, the loved Guinea pig would have been lifted up above the teeth. The poor little guy needed to be lifted up because the threat was real.

Something was on the prowl that wanted to eat him. Satan is not about warnings. No friendly sniffing to give us time to react. Wham! Fangs.

Pray:

I confess that when I fail to lift others up in prayer it is because I have allowed my cares to center around me. I have too often been lulled into a sense of comfort, forgetting there is a roaring lion that wants to devour me, my brothers, and my sisters. Remind me, Father, that the threats are real and restore a love in me for everyone.

Since you have purified your souls in obeying the truth
through the Spirit in sincere love of the brethren,
love one another fervently with a pure heart.
(1 Peter 1:22)

-26-

WHERE HAVE YOU BEEN?

I remember waiting up at night when I would hear that this young new standup comic would be on the Johnny Carson show. His name was Jerry Seinfeld. He went on to have a successful career after that, I believe. I remember him talking about dogs having no sense of time. You could be gone from home for ten days or ten minutes, and you'd get the same excited greeting. It was a funny routine that you would have to see to appreciate, but he was right. Dogs are so excited to see you no matter how long you have been gone, exactly like they have no sense of time.

However, you know your dog has an amazing sense of time. I don't think dogs react like that because they don't know the difference between days and minutes. In The Social Wolf, an article from the website Living with Wolves, this is related:

> *In the winter of 2005, the alpha female of the Toklat Pack was caught in a snare. Two other females from the pack stuck with their pack leader, who was also likely their mother and*

> *were eventually trapped as well. After these wolves were killed, the alpha male returned for months to this spot until he too was killed by a hunter.*

My guess is that dogs, being pack-oriented creatures, are just not accustomed to pack members leaving for any amount of time.

> *...A lone wolf is a wolf that is searching, and what it seeks is another wolf. Everything in a wolf's nature tells it to belong to something greater than itself: a pack. Like us, wolves form friendships and maintain lifelong bonds. They succeed by cooperating, and they struggle when they're alone. Like us, wolves need one another. ...*

I wonder if our dogs greet us each time because they don't process us leaving for any good reason. Though wolves do leave the pack according to this article (instinct drives that to keep the DNA fresh), it is not an everyday occurrence. It may be that our dogs cannot understand leaving in the same way we do and never will be able to do so.

I believe from my scripture reading that Jesus loves the Church, His bride, so much that this is not far off from the spirit we are to have for one another. This may be a warning to you. A serious warning, maybe a little scarier for you than any of the other devotionals in this book.

Do you care about the pack? Do you care about a pack member straying away? If not, are you really a pack member or just hanging out? If you remember the Devotion on Big Dogs and Little Dogs, this is a big dog if you don't.

1 Peter 1:22 tells Christians, "Since you have purified your souls in obeying the truth through the Spirit in sincere love of the brethren, love one another fervently with a pure heart" (emphasis added). That about says it all. Note the strong word **"fervently."** We should all ask ourselves if our prayer is truly fervent.

Pray:

Father, let my love for my brothers and sisters be real. May I love each member of my family in Christ so much that they matter to me deeply. If I am failing in this area, please help me to repent and be aligned with You.

Let each of you look out not only for his own interests,
but also for the interests of others.
(Philippians 2:4)

-27-

Hey, Get off There

W e obtained a rescue kitten I named Bonhoeffer. He was the best cat we ever owned. Our cats are outdoor cats but get a lot of attention and care. Rattlesnakes are not uncommon for us, so having a cat in the area really does help. Bonhoeffer and Kyle wrestled and played like they were both dogs. They even cuddled together.

One day, that kitten climbed on top of Kyle's doghouse. Kyle is big, muscular, and tough as nails. When you look straight at him, his jowls were Rottweiler. This dog sees kitten Bonhoeffer up there and responds by engulfing Bonhoeffer in his mouth and gently as a surgeon placing him on the ground.

Kyle was being so motherly to that kitten. What a protector. He did not want the kitten to get hurt up there. It was so funny to see a kitten almost disappear in a mouth that could bite it in half and gulp it down in two.

What a great picture for us when we see someone in danger or in need.

What can this look like?

At the workplace, we are often dealing with coworkers who are not operating at a healthy performance level. Sometimes, the person is being lazy, and the poor performance is volitional. Other times, the person may just not have the skills, knowledge, or ability to meet the needs.

Whatever the case, they are on the top of the doghouse and need help. That is true even if they put themselves there through their own fault.

One response is to be in the sea of fellow employees complaining about the person in the break room. The other response is to gently help the person out of the problem, even if it means an uncomfortable conversion or confrontation.

At home, we can have people on the top of a doghouse. Life presents all sorts of challenges at home, and it is easy to just ignore all of them. Raising kids takes a lot of effort, and life is hard enough. Can't we just let ignore someone in need and let them figure it out themselves? While there may be times it is best to let someone struggle through something, the decision to do so should not be because we don't care enough, or we don't feel like helping. We should not snap at someone with a sharp tongue with no intention of helping them.

Kyle showed us. He saw a risk, he saw a need, and he gently addressed the need.

Pray:

Father, allow us the wisdom to know who to help and when to help them. Give us a caring spirit for people who need a gentle lift. Open opportunities for us to provide help to others in Your name.

"If you love me, keep my commandments."
— Jesus in John 14:15

Now That Is Obedience

I would describe Kyle as a bird dog if I had to describe him for his prominent aptitude. He could do a number of things well if he were to be made into a working dog, but his most apparent ability was bird hunting. Our daily walk included quail and turkey areas. Kyle was very good at flushing both. I am not a hunter, but my friend took him pheasant hunting and yes, he came back with a pheasant and a good report.

Then, we did something almost cruel. We capitulated to our daughter's begging and got some chicks, raised them in the garage until big enough to face the world, and then we moved them outside. We wanted free-range chickens, but we did have to surmount a dog problem. We had a dog passionate about catching birds.

Two chickens in a backyard were hardly sporting, but Kyle didn't mind. He looked appreciative for bringing him a lunch so fresh it was still walking. However, I knew Kyle really wanted to please me and normally would not do anything he understood to be wrong. "Understood" is the key word here. It took a while for Kyle to understand the unbelievable. I didn't want the chickens caught, killed, and eaten. Incredible! Inconceivable to him at first.

A few days of not letting Kyle in the backyard unless I had him on a leash was all that was needed. I would take him near the chickens and tell him no when he started to sharpen his knives and put a napkin under his collar. Kyle would look back at me in wonderment. Eventually, the leash came off and close monitoring occurred. Soon after that, nothing could cause Kyle to hurt those chickens. He was obedient once it was clear to him that we did not want those chickens dead.

Often, Jesus said things so simple His message was jarring. He said in John 14:15, "If you love me, keep my commandments."

When meditating on a verse I sometimes flip it. In this case, I ask myself, "If I don't keep His commands, does that mean I don't love Him?" That was a powerful meditation that led me to a confession. If I thought God was not forgiving, if I thought the cross was too small to handle my sins, or that my salvation was dependent on my willpower, I would run from this verse.

- *Are you overestimating your love of Jesus?*
- *Are you afraid to confess a lack of love for Jesus?*
- *Are you afraid to explore where you are not obedient because it may rock your world?*

Pray:

Jesus, please don't let me shrink from confession, even if it means I am confessing I don't love You as I should. Thank You for loving me even during those times my love for You is so weak when compared to Yours.

...backbiters, haters of God, violent, proud, boasters, inventors of evil things, disobedient to parents, undiscerning, untrustworthy, unloving, unforgiving, unmerciful; who, knowing the righteous judgment of God, that those who practice such things are deserving of death, not only do the same but also approve of those who practice them.
(Romans 1:30-32)

OH, PLEASE DON'T ROLL IN THAT

J osi and Dusty. We loved them. No kids, so we took them everywhere.

We visited the family of in-laws once and took our girls. Josi and Dusty were fine anywhere we went staying in the truck. These folks lived in a country setting so we were sure to find our beloved dogs some fun places to take them exploring. Notice though, we were visiting family of in-laws. These awesome folks were hosting us for an afternoon, but we were not related and did not know them extremely well.

Our host took us out to his property for a walk and showed us around. He was particularly proud of his chickens. They had bonded with him and were good layers.

After the tour, we were all going to go somewhere so we were going to leave our dogs in the truck. I don't exactly remember how it came about, but our host offered to let our dogs stay in his large, fenced area. We took him up on that and left. We should have never returned.

Arriving back and approaching our dogs in the fenced area, we began to sense something was wrong. It was the feathers. Lots of feathers. The closer we walked to the enclosure the more feathers we saw. Ultimately, the carnage was upon us. Two chickens were surgically de-breasted. I guess our dogs didn't like dark meat. As we all stood there, our host's face was ashen.

He was too good a man to make us feel bad, but it was obvious that sadness was upon him.

Then it happened. Our inappropriately frisky and proud dogs came up to us. Dusty laid down at our host's feet and began rolling on her back on top of one of the victims and Dusty even put one of her legs against our host's legs. He probably wanted to kick her. Gosh, even I wanted to kick her. So embarrassing!

Chapter 1 of Romans is not likely to be on a corporate website. The reason being that it lists what God hates, and does not hold back. Very politically incorrect, not to mention it could make us all feel bad. Making people feel bad is bad, according to our current culture. In verse 32, Paul speaks of the wicked knowing "...the righteous judgment of God, that those who practice such things are deserving of death, not only do the same but also approve of those who practice them." Paul is describing not chicken killers, but chicken killers who roll in their kill. These folks love their sins. They encourage them.

No wonder Christians will always be hated by so many. We know what we have done is worthy of death. We don't white-wash the sins nor deny our part in them. We confess them. We repent of them. We are broken because of our sins. We recognize we are hopeless and dead without the Cross.

People who roll in them are not interested in hearing the good news of the Cross. It might make them feel bad.

Pray:

Lord, we know this world hates You and Your children. So many hate Your messages and warnings. Let us love our enemies and communicate love to even those who do not understand their wrongs. May they see You soon, repent of their sins, and fall at the foot of the cross with us.

And God will wipe away every tear from their eyes;
there shall be no more death, nor sorrow, nor crying.
There shall be no more pain,
for the former things have passed away.
(Revelation 21:4)

-30-

WHERE DID THE TIME GO?

In 1969, I was a three-year-old walking into a pound on Camp Mercy in Okinawa. Though young, I remember it well. She barked at us in a friendly "pick me" way and wagged her tail. She failed to mention we would never be able to domesticate her, and we would have to live on her terms from now on. You guessed it-Tinker. We selected her. She was beautiful. At about 35 pounds, she had a healthy build and gorgeous multicolored fur. Bright white with rich mahogany browns. Flopped over years. Classic Japanese curly-tail.

In 1985, I returned home to visit from my freshman year of college. Tinker was gone. I knew she would not be there. She was skeletal that last time I was home. I knew my parents would not tell me if she died when I was away at school, and I purposely never asked about her. We all knew this was best. The house was so empty without her. I had no memory of life without her.

I cried that day and night-a lot. Reflecting on all this, I am crying now, decades later. However, I would not trade one tear for not having had Tinker, my other dogs, or my parents who I lost in the same year three years ago. It's looking like the country I grew up in might be gone soon, too. I remember from C.S. Lewis that the pain of loss is a sign that you had a great blessing.

Dear reader, do not lose hope. Hold on to the promise in Revelation 21:4. We can see the pain of this world for what it is only because God has allowed us to glimpse things that are good and shadows of what things should have been all along. Do not give up. No other faith has the hope we have. Jesus stands alone in presenting the unvarnished, painful truth about us and this world, and also fulfilling the promise of eternal joy and no more tears.

My Prayer for You

Father, watch over this precious person. Guard this person's heart with all mercy. Give this Christian a heart to pursue You to the end of life on earth when mourning ceases, nothing hurts, and we can all finally see Your face.

Then to Adam He said, "Because you have heeded the voice of your wife, and have eaten from the tree of which I commanded you, saying, 'You shall not eat of it':
"Cursed is the ground for your sake; in toil you shall eat of it all the days of your life. Both thorns and thistles it shall bring forth for you, and you shall eat the herb of the field.
In the sweat of your face you shall eat bread till you return to the ground, for out of it you were taken; for dust you are, And to dust you shall return.
(Genesis 3:17-19)

LIFE IS SHORT AND IT'S MY FAULT

A few short days ago, I put Kyle down and yes, I am crying as I write this. I started this book several years ago more as a journal to capture thoughts for perhaps my kids or grandkids. Then, I thought perhaps I could put them in a devotional when I had time after retirement. So, I am retired, and I don't have Kyle or any other dog for that matter. It is too soon.

I can't go into veterinary offices to put my dogs down. I have them come out to my car. I don't cry a little. I cry a lot. I sob. My nose runs like a spigot. I get it from my dad. He was a crier, too. As I sat holding Kyle as he was being injected, all I could say was "I'm sorry." Over and over again. Through the burial. Driving away. The next day. "I'm so sorry buddy. It's my fault."

He died a natural death. I didn't run over him or anything. His death wasn't my fault in that direct sense. I wasn't sorry for putting him down because it was the right thing to do. He was old for his breed and suffering. So, what was I sorry for? Why was it my fault?

The history of mankind started in the Garden of Eden. It is now referred to often as "Paradise Lost." Adam and Eve both chose to take their hand at being God, therefore, many things changed. The bell could not be "unrung."

Paradise was lost. Diseases, accidents, murders (very soon thereafter actually), wars, famine, and everything bad we have names for began there. It would be nice if we could corporately blame our parents, Adam and Eve, but the longer we live and the more we grow we see the desire in our souls for control. We can make the decisions. We can be as God. How well has that worked out?

So, I feel my sentiment in apologizing to Kyle was correct. My people sinned. We lost a paradise where dogs don't get cancer. Where they don't become crippled from hip dysplasia. Where they don't get hit by cars. Where they don't have to be given away because their beloved human dies or cannot take care of them anymore for health or economic reasons. Adam was first charged with the care of the animals in the Garden. They mattered to God.

So, when a dog in your life passes, it is okay to be broken. Voddie Baucham gives a knock-out sermon on brokenness.[17] You would be well served to find it.

While we are not to mope around in a joyless life, beating ourselves up with guilt or despair, we are not to ignore the real-time results of our sins playing out all around us. When you watch one of those commercials for a charity serving children with severe medical needs, it is okay to say "I'm sorry" to yourself. We all had a hand in this.

You may be a young Christian or perhaps you are not a Christian, so this idea of feeling the responsibility for Paradise

Lost may not be sounding right to you. Maybe it does sound right to be fighting it. However, older Christians know we need not look any further for answers as to why bad things are happening than our own hearts. The same choices in the hearts of Adam and Eve are in me.

"I am sorry Kyle. It's my fault."

Pray:

Father, I acknowledge that the same sinful desire that caused many great grandparents to fall also lives in me. I am guilty of taking something wonderful and breaking it badly. May I never pridefully put myself above anyone else. Please kill the pride in me that started this mess we live in now and caused even animals to suffer. Thank You for the day where the lion will once again lay with the lamb.

THE DOGS

Kyle

Tinker and Me

Josie and Dusty

Tag

Jersey

Endnotes

1 https://www.goodreads.com/author/
quotes/1082290.A_W_Tozer, author of "The
Pursuit of God"

2 lindawillows.com › 2021/07/29 › face-to-face-with
"Face to Face with God", Quotes from D. Martin
Lloyd-Jones …

3 Goodreads.com

4 Goodreads.com

5 Charles Spurgeon Quotes Christianquotes.info

6 Goodreads.com

7 www.crosswalk.com

8 www.christianquotes.info › top-quotes ›

9 www.christianquotes.info

10 https://www.christianquotes.info/quotes-by-topic/
quotes-about-fear/

[11] Tozer, Aiden Wilson. The Pursuit of God (Updated, Annotated) (p. 97). Aneko Press. Kindle Edition

[12] https://www.desiringgod.org/interviews/is-god-a-megalomaniac

[13] www.azquotes.com > quotes > topics

[14] https://www.desiringgod.org/articles/holy-play *A Christian Theology of Sport And Competition* August 24, 2021

[15] Goodreads.com

[16] Goodreads.com

[17] Voddie Baucham: Brokenness - Bing video

Lightning Source UK Ltd.
Milton Keynes UK
UKHW011327080223
416610UK00017B/2366